TUTANKHAMUN
ULTIMATE ACTIVITY BOOK

HENDRIKJE NOUWENS

ILLUSTRATIONS BY MARTIN HENSE

THE BRITISH MUSEUM PRESS

Some material originally published in the Netherlands in 2000 by Barjesteh van Waalwijk van Doorn & Co's Uitgeversmaatschappij.
© Copyright 2000 by Barjesteh van Waalwijk van Doorn & Co's Uitgeversmaatschappij.

This edition first published in 2007 by British Museum Press
A division of The British Museum Company Ltd, 38 Russell Square, London WC1B 3QQ

Second impression 2008

ISBN   978-0-7141-3038-5

A catalogue record for this title is available from the British Library.

This edition designed and typeset by Herringbone Design.
Printed and bound by Tien Wah Pte Ltd, Malaysia.

CONTENTS

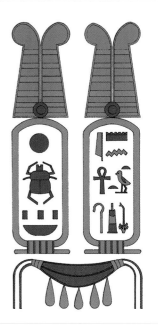

1 TUTANKHAMUN, THE BOY KING 4
WRITE A LETTER TO TUTANKHAMUN IN HIEROGLYPHS 6

2 THE DISCOVERY OF A LOST ROYAL TOMB 8
PLAY THE TUTANKHAMUN CARD GAME 12

3 A TOMB FULL OF TREASURES 14
MAKE A MODEL OF TUTANKHAMUN'S TOMB 20

4 TUTANKHAMUN'S WARDROBE 22
5 ANCIENT EGYPTIAN FASHION 24

MAKE YOUR OWN EGYPTIAN TUNIC AND SASH 26

6 SHOES, HAIR AND BEAUTY 28

MAKE YOUR OWN EGYPTIAN JEWELLERY 32

ACTIVITY SHEETS 1–8

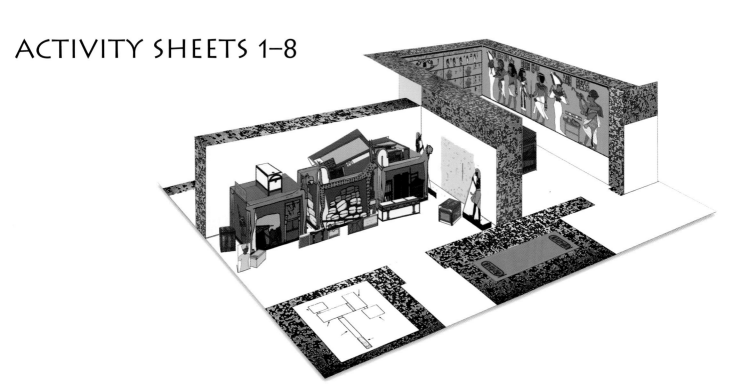

TUTANKHAMUN, THE BOY KING

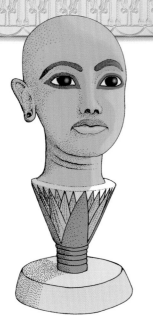

Tutankhamun became pharaoh of Egypt in around 1336 BC, two years after his father, Akhenaten, died. Tutankhamun was only nine years old. Imagine becoming king at only nine! Tutankhamun had to take many important decisions. The king had to command the Egyptian army, control the finances of the country, and administer justice. His people also expected him to make offerings to the gods in the temples. He had officials to help, but it must have been a very difficult job.

Tutankhamun.

TUTANKHAMUN'S FAMILY

King Akhenaten had two wives, Nefertiti and Kiya. Egyptian pharaohs were allowed to marry more than once. Akhenaten and his chief wife Nefertiti had six daughters but no sons. Akhenaten's secondary wife Kiya was probably Tutankhamun's mother.

The young Tutankhamun married his half-sister, Ankhesenamun.

Nefertiti, chief wife of Akhenaten.

Kiya, secondary wife of Akhenaten.

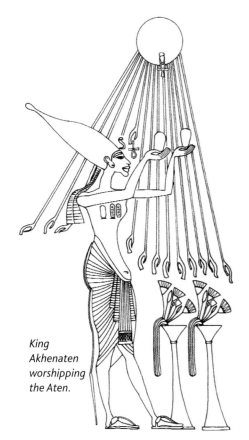

King Akhenaten worshipping the Aten.

THE GOD ATEN

When Tutankhamun was born, his parents named him Tut-ankh-Aten. This means 'living image of the Aten'. The Aten was the god of the sun. This deity was pictured as a sun disc with long rays ending in hands. Akhenaten worshipped this god alone, and rejected all the other gods of Egypt.

King Akhenaten had many new temples built. They were large sanctuaries with long rows of altars, and they were all meant for the worship of the sun god Aten. Akhenaten closed the temples of the other gods. The pharaoh also had all the names and statues of the other gods removed and destroyed, even those of the great god Amun. Amun was the most important god of Thebes and he was worshipped by many Egyptians. The priests of Amun were furious!

A NEW CAPITAL CITY

Akhenaten also built a beautiful new capital city. He chose a very special place in the desert, at a site now known as el-Amarna. He called his new city Akhetaten, 'horizon of the Aten'. Tutankhamun was probably born there.

GREAT CHANGES

After Akhenaten's death there were many changes. The new young king decided that everybody in the country was allowed to believe in more than one god, just as they had before his father ruled Egypt. Tutankhamun therefore abolished the Aten religion, and the old religion with many gods took its place. The temples which had been closed by Akhenaten were reopened under the new king. Tutankhamun also decided to move the royal court to Memphis. The town of Thebes became the religious centre of the country once again. And Tutankhamun changed his name. Tut-ankh-Aten became Tut-ankh-Amun (Tutankhamun): 'living image of the Amun'. Amun was restored as the great god of Egypt.

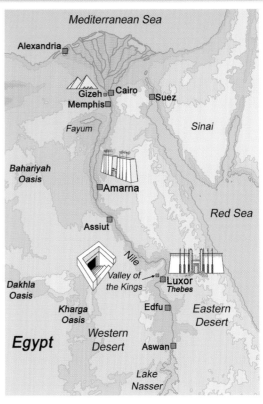

Map of Egypt.

Statue of Tutankhamun.

THE DEATH OF THE KING

It is the year 1323 BC. Nobody is working in Egypt. Parties are cancelled, banquets are postponed. It has been announced that King Tutankhamun has died. At his funeral, wailing women throw sand over their heads and make a shrieking sound of grief.

The rule of Tutankhamun came to an abrupt end with his death. The king was only eighteen years old. As Tutankhamun and his wife had no children, Ay succeeded the deceased king. Ay was the vizier, a high official, who had assisted Tutankhamun during his reign. The new king even married the young widow of Tutankhamun.

Nobody knows how Tutankhamun died. His mummy shows traces of a kind of head wound, so some people say that he was murdered. Perhaps Ay wanted to take power and struck Tutankhamun a blow to the back of his head. It is also possible, of course, that Tutankhamun fell from his chariot by accident during a lion hunt. He cannot tell us …

An ancient Egyptian funeral procession.

WRITE A LETTER TO TUTANKHAMUN IN HIEROGLYPHS

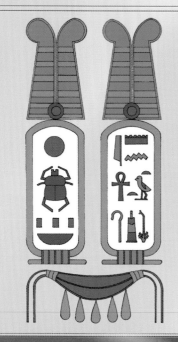

Over 5000 years ago the people of Egypt started to use writing. However, they did not use letters like ours. The ancient Egyptians used picture-signs that looked like plants, people, animals and objects. These picture-signs are called hieroglyphs. At first, every drawing represented an entire word. If an Egyptian writer wanted to write 'arm' then he drew a picture of an arm. Later this changed and some of the pictures represented sounds as well.

The Egyptians often carved their texts into the stone walls of temples. Many texts in ancient Egypt were also written on papyrus. This writing material was made of the stalks of the papyrus, a plant that grew along the river Nile. The ancient Egyptians used a reed pen and red or black paint for writing on the strong papyrus sheets.

An Egyptian scribe.

YOU WILL NEED

A black pen.

You may also want colouring pencils or felt-tip pens, a sheet of white paper, and scissors.

On the page opposite you will see a sheet of papyrus and a list that shows you how to write some useful words and numbers in hieroglyphic script. There is also a list of hieroglyphs that write the sounds of single letters, so that you can spell out other words.

Use the lists to write your letter to Tutankhamun. Decide what you want to say, and practise writing your message in hieroglyphs on a spare piece of paper. You might tell the king what your name is and how old you are, whether you have brothers and sisters, where you live and what your hobbies are.

When you are happy with your hieroglyphic letter, write a neat copy on the scroll provided. The cartouche (oval ring) is for the name of Tutankhamun. In ancient Egypt the name of the king was always written in a cartouche.

HINTS
• Use a black pen to write your letter.

• Do not forget to look at the hieroglyphs in the list of words and numbers on page 7.

• Try different ways to write the hieroglyphs. Egyptians wrote from left to right or from right to left, and also from top to bottom. You could make the hieroglyphs a bit bigger and colour them in.

• Write your own name in a royal cartouche. Trace the cartouche on the page opposite. Write your name, spelling out the sounds with hieroglyphs. If you enlarge the cartouche and cut it out, you can use it as a badge or a name-plate.

a	vulture or arm	j	snake	r	mouth
b	leg	k	basket	s	folded cloth
c	*see* k *or* s	l	lion	t	bread
d	hand	m	owl	u	quail chick
e, ee	reed	n	water	v	horned viper
f	horned viper	o	quail chick	w	quail chick
g	jar-stand	p	stool	x	basket and cloth
h	house	q	hillside	y	reeds z	bolt
i	reed				

EGYPTIAN VOCABULARY

I   you (male) (female)

king   family

father   mother

brother   sister

country   Egypt

town   street

palace   house

month   day

big   little

good   bad

to, for (a person)   to, for (a place)

in, out (of)   with

go, walk   sit; live (somewhere)

1 | 2 || 10 ∩   17 ∩|||| 320 ∩∩∩   100 ℰ   1,000

3 ||| 11 ∩| 100 ℰ   1,000

Tutankhamun

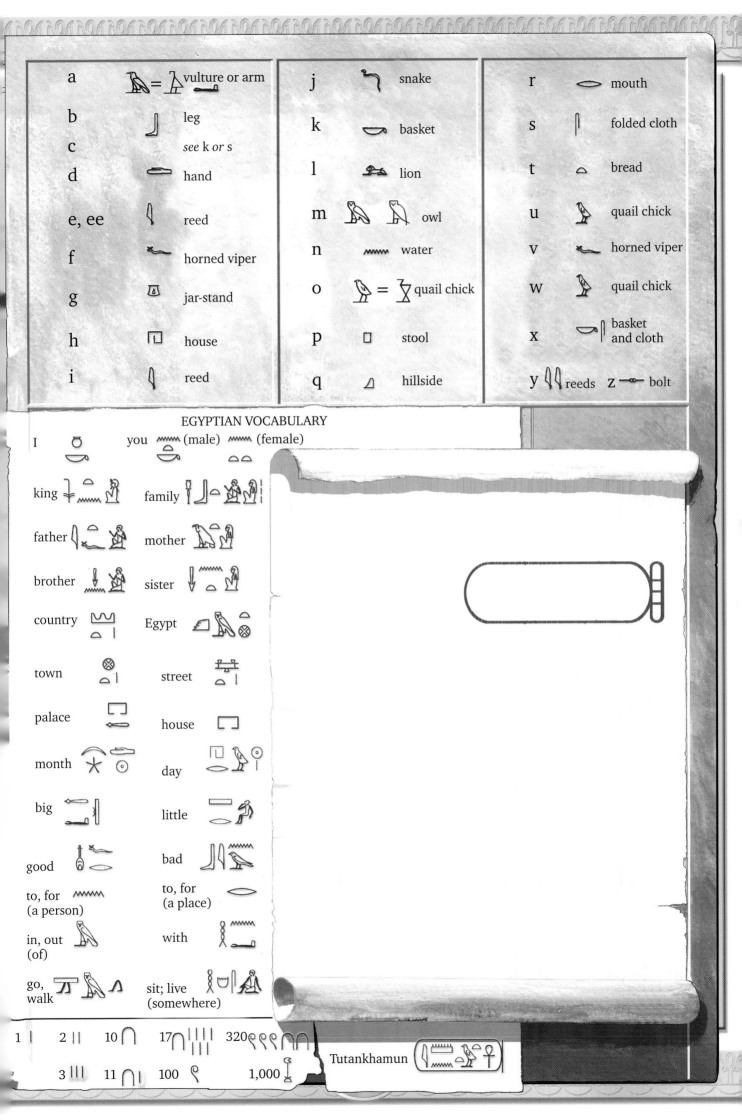

THE DISCOVERY OF A LOST ROYAL TOMB

Every year, many tourists in Egypt visit the Valley of the Kings. This valley is near the old city of Thebes (modern Luxor), on the west bank of the river Nile. Here the tombs of many ancient Egyptian kings have been cut into the cliffs. All these rulers lived in a period which Egyptologists call the New Kingdom, which lasted from about 1550 to 1070 BC. King Tutankhamun had his own rock-cut tomb in the Valley.

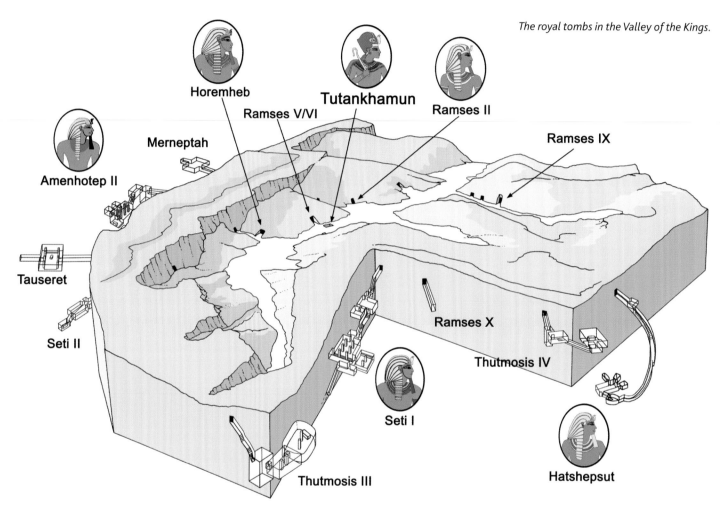

The royal tombs in the Valley of the Kings.

Horemheb

Ramses V/VI

Tutankhamun

Ramses II

Merneptah

Amenhotep II

Ramses IX

Tauseret

Seti II

Ramses X

Thutmosis IV

Seti I

Thutmosis III

Hatshepsut

EXCAVATIONS IN THE VALLEY OF THE KINGS

Many archaeologists (people who study the remains of the past) were working in the Valley of the Kings in the 19th and 20th centuries. They came from different countries to find the tombs of the rulers of the New Kingdom and learn more about life in ancient Egypt. However, they soon found that many of the royal tombs in the Valley had been looted in ancient times. Robbers had stolen the valuable objects that were buried with the pharaohs. Therefore, the archaeologists found only a few objects in most of the tombs.

After many seasons of excavations, nearly everyone was convinced that there was nothing new to be discovered in the Valley of the Kings. In 1914 the American Theodore Davis decided that he had had enough. He did not renew his permit to excavate in the Valley. There was, however, a stubborn archaeologist who thought that one more royal tomb was still hidden in the Valley.

HOWARD CARTER

That man was Howard Carter, an Englishman born in London on 9th May, 1874. Carter had a talent for drawing, and when he was fifteen years old he started to earn money by painting portraits of parrots, cats and lap dogs. In September 1891, the young Carter found himself working in Egypt as a draughtsman, copying ancient Egyptian paintings and texts. But he also gained experience in archaeological digging work and worked as an inspector of the Service of Antiquities. In 1909 Carter met the Earl of Carnarvon. This rich nobleman was very interested in ancient Egypt. After the departure of Theodore Davis, Carnarvon got permission to begin an excavation in the Valley of the Kings. In the autumn of 1917 Carter and his friend Carnarvon, who supplied the money, started their search for the tomb of Tutankhamun.

Howard Carter.

THE LAST CHANCE

Five years passed without success for Carter and Carnarvon. It was a desperate situation. The excavations in the Valley of the Kings were a huge expense. In the end Carnarvon lost his nerve. In the summer of 1922, Carnarvon told Carter that he could no longer afford to continue the excavations. It was a tremendous disappointment for the archaeologist, but he was determined to continue. 'Then I'll pay for the excavation myself,' Carter is supposed to have said. The Earl of Carnarvon was so impressed that he promised to give his friend one last chance.

In November 1922 Carter was ready to start on the last excavation season sponsored by Carnarvon. However, where should he excavate? Nearly all the likely places in the Valley of the Kings had already been investigated. In the end Carter decided to try his luck close to the entrance to the tomb of King Ramses VI. It was his last chance to find Tutankhamun's grave.

At that spot, there were a number of huts of the workmen who had worked 3,000 years earlier on the tomb of Ramses VI. On 3rd November Carter's fifty Egyptian labourers started to remove these huts. On 4th November the unexpected happened. When the archaeologist arrived on site that morning, it was unusually quiet. It soon became clear to Carter that something special must have happened. And yes, under the first hut a stone step had been discovered!

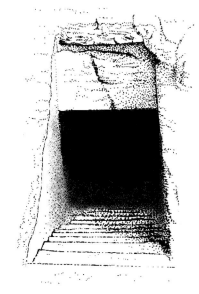

For the rest of the day and the next morning, the excavations continued feverishly. The tension was enormous. Step after step appeared from under the sand. Could this tomb have been used to bury a king? Had the tomb been looted by robbers, like so many of the other tombs in the Valley? Excited, Carter watched the digging of the Egyptian labourers. Now the work progressed with great speed. On 5th November, towards dusk, the top of a sealed entrance door became visible. A superb find! Would Carter's years of patient labour in the Valley be rewarded after all?

The entrance to the tomb.

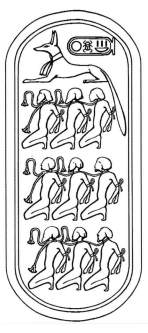

THE GREAT DISCOVERY

Although Carter could not see the name of the owner of the tomb on the seals of the door, it soon became clear that it was a royal tomb. Could this be the grave for which he had been looking all these years? Carter had a difficult decision to make. Of course, Carter wanted to continue the excavations immediately. However, the Earl of Carnarvon, the nobleman who had paid for Carter's excavations, was still in England. The archaeologist decided to temporarily close the entrance to the tomb and to send his friend a telegram. In this message he told the earl of the remarkable discovery. On 23th November Carnarvon arrived in Luxor with his daughter Evelyn. The next day, the sixteen stone steps to the entrance of the tomb were cleared again. Slowly the whole door became visible. The great moment had arrived. On the seals at the bottom of the door the men discovered the name of King Tutankhamun.

The seals on the entrance door of Tutankhamun's tomb.

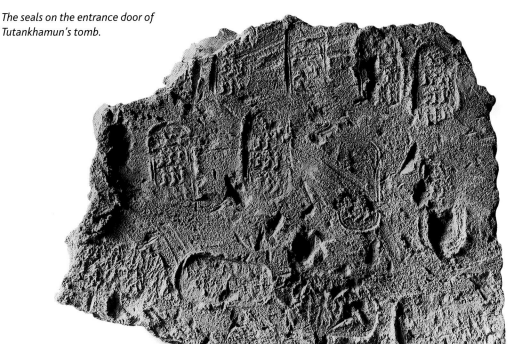

Now Howard Carter and the Earl of Carnarvon knew for certain that they had found Tutankhamun's grave. But the sealed door showed traces of a break-in. Had the grave been plundered by ancient robbers, after all? The excavators quickly resumed their work. Behind the entrance door a downward-sloping corridor became visible, completely filled with rubble. And then they saw yet another plastered and sealed entrance. With trembling hands Carter managed to make a small hole in the top left-hand corner of this second door. Everybody held their breath. It was dark in the tomb and some hot air escaped. Then Carter enlarged the opening, slipped his candle through the hole and looked inside. Slowly he let his eyes get accustomed to the dim light.

The flame of the candle flickered and then … Carter could not believe his eyes. He saw a room full of the most beautiful objects. A real treasure-house!

Beds in the shape of enormous, strange animals cast their shadows on the walls of the room. Next some chariot wheels, painted chests and two life-size statues appeared from the gloom. And the glitter of gold was visible everywhere. It was the impatient Carnarvon who broke the expectant silence. 'Can you see anything?' he asked Carter. 'Yes, wonderful things,' was his answer. The tomb of Tutankhamun had finally been found.

Carter opens the second sealed door of the royal tomb.

The first glimpse of the antechamber.

PLAY THE TUTANKHAMUN CARD GAME

YOU WILL NEED

The cards from Activity sheets 1, 2 and 3.

ENTERTAINMENT

In the tomb of Tutankhamun there were many objects for the king to use in the afterlife, such as beds, chairs, stools and linen. Tutankhamun also had several games placed in his tomb so that he would not get bored in the afterlife.

TUTANKHAMUN — Tutankhamun
Became King of Egypt at the age of nine. Ruled from 1333 to 1323 BC. Made Memphis the capital again and restored many temples.
Ankhesenamun - Kiya - Akhenaten

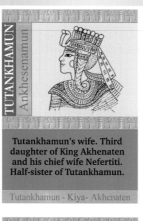

TUTANKHAMUN — Ankhesenamun
Tutankhamun's wife. Third daughter of King Akhenaten and his chief wife Nefertiti. Half-sister of Tutankhamun.
Tutankhamun - Kiya - Akhenaten

TUTANKHAMUN — Akhenaten
Tutankhamun's wives were Nefe... Ruled from 135... Worshipped o... Built the city...
Tutankhamun...

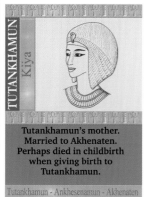

TUTANKHAMUN — Kiya
Tutankhamun's mother. Married to Akhenaten. Perhaps died in childbirth when giving birth to Tutankhamun.
Tutankhamun - Ankhesenamun - Akhenaten

EGYPTIAN GODS — Anubis
God of the dead. Pictured as a jackal or with a jackal's head. Supervised the mummification of the dead.
Osiris - Nut - Horus

GOLDEN TREASURES — Golden mask
Made of solid gold, inlaid with coloured glass and semi-precious stones. It was placed over the head of the young king. It weighs about 11 kg and is 54 cm
sceptre...

MORE TREASURES — Ritual bed
Animal-shaped bed from the antechamber of the tomb. The pharaoh's soul could rest on this bed during the journey to the afterlife.
chariot - statue

APPEARANCE — Bracelet
Bracelet with scarab beetles made of dark-blue lapis lazuli. The scarabs were the symbol of rebirth and life after death.
sandals - unguent jar - pectoral

On Activity sheets 1, 2 and 3 you will find 32 playing cards. These belong to the Tutankhamun Card Game.

Carefully press out the cards and put them in a pile.

RULES OF THE GAME

The game is best with 3 or more players.

The Tutankhamun Card Game consists of eight sets or 'families' of four cards. Every set has its own colour. The aim of the game is to collect the largest number of complete sets, by asking other players for cards.

The dealer shuffles the cards then deals them all out face down. The player on the dealer's left begins. The player decides which card he or she needs to complete a set and asks another player for that card.

IMPORTANT: you are not allowed to ask for a card unless you already hold one or more cards from that set.

If the second player has the card he or she must hand it over and the first player then has another turn. The first player can ask any other player for a card. When a player is asked for a card but does not have it, then the turn passes to that player.

As soon as a player collects a set of four cards, he or she must show the set to the other players and lay it out on the table. When a player has no more cards, he or she is out. The other players continue until no player has any cards left. The winner is the player with the most complete sets.

QUIZ GAME

You can also use the Tutankhamun Cards for a quiz game. One player acts as quizmaster and uses the information on the cards to ask questions about the life of Tutankhamun, the discovery of his tomb, or about the objects found in the tomb.

For instance: when was Tutankhamun king of Egypt? Who was the Earl of Carnarvon? How many kilos does the king's golden funerary mask weigh? What is pictured on Tutankhamun's wooden sandals?

If the question is answered correctly, the quizmaster hands over the card and the same player can have another question. If the answer is wrong, somebody else gets a new question. The player with the most cards at the end of the quiz is the winner.

Nut

Goddess of the sky. Often painted blue and covered with stars. Each evening she swallows the sun, which is born again the next morning.

Osiris - Anubis - Horus

EGYPTIAN GODS

Horus

God shown as a falcon or with a falcon's head. Every king is thought to be a Horus on earth and therefore a god.

Osiris - Anubis - Nut

A TOMB FULL OF TREASURES

THE ANTECHAMBER

Howard Carter and the Earl of Carnarvon had made the most sensational discovery of the 20th century: a royal tomb with many splendid objects still inside. When Carter got over the first shock, he enlarged the hole in the entrance door to the tomb. Vases of translucent alabaster, wooden stools, a throne inlaid with gold and semi-precious stones, a heap of white oval boxes … The tomb looked like a museum! If there had been thieves, they must have been disturbed during their work. The two gentlemen could not believe their luck. So many treasures! Slowly it dawned on Carter and Carnarvon that this could not be the only room in the tomb. No mummy or coffin was to be seen among the chaotically stacked, colourful collection of objects. Eventually the researchers discovered another sealed door in the right-hand side of the antechamber. That had to be the burial chamber.

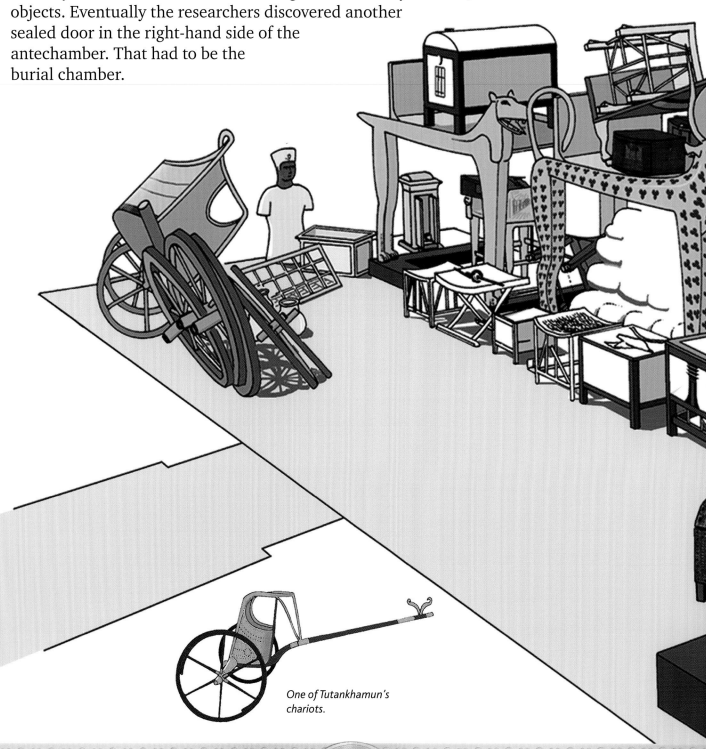

One of Tutankhamun's chariots.

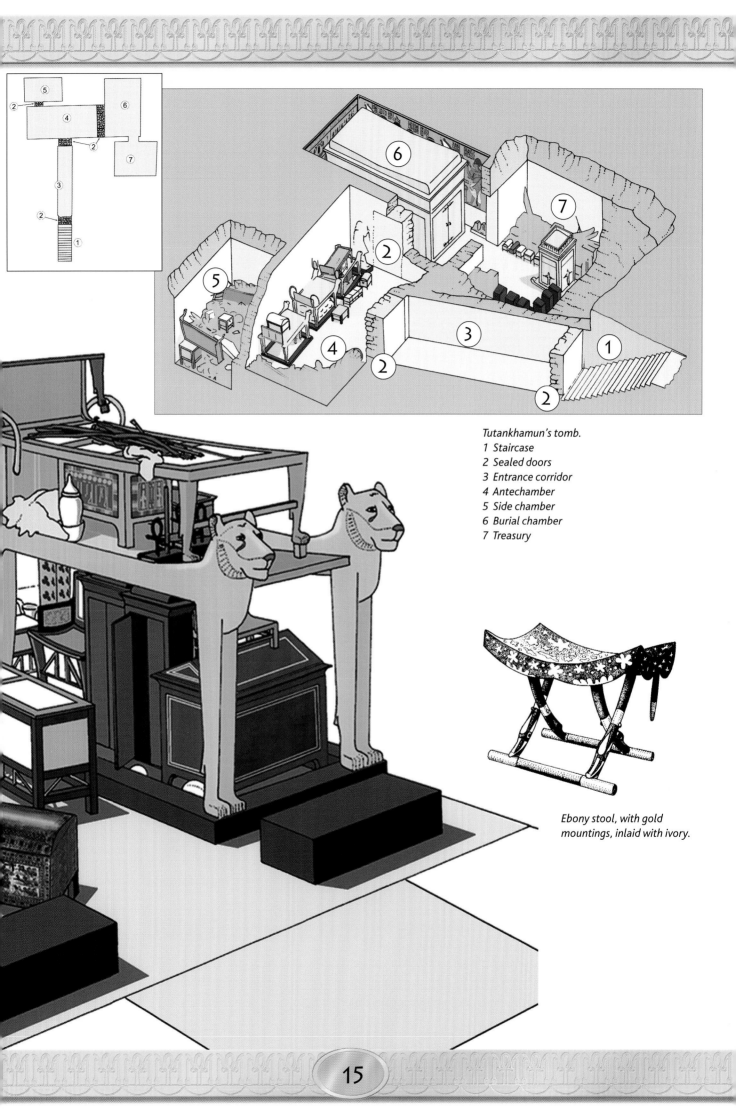

Tutankhamun's tomb.
1 Staircase
2 Sealed doors
3 Entrance corridor
4 Antechamber
5 Side chamber
6 Burial chamber
7 Treasury

Ebony stool, with gold mountings, inlaid with ivory.

WORLD NEWS

On Thursday 30th November 1922, the London newspaper 'The Times' reported the news of the spectacular tomb find. The newspaper proudly announced that the Earl of Carnarvon and Howard Carter, after many years of searching, had discovered the tomb of King Tutankhamun in the Valley of the Kings. From that moment onwards the whole world thrilled with the excavators. Many congratulatory telegrams and letters flooded into the small post office in Luxor. Large groups of tourists showed up in the Valley of the Kings hoping to catch a glimpse of Howard Carter. Souvenir hunters besieged the entrance of the tomb. But Carter knew that he had to remain calm. The archaeologist asked a few colleagues to help him and patiently and very meticulously they started to clear out the antechamber. They numbered every object, then photographed it in its original position and described it. Then the finds were treated, packed and one at a time brought to a laboratory. This was set up in the nearby tomb of King Seti II.

Carnarvon and Carter at the entrance of Tutankhamun's burial chamber.

THE BURIAL CHAMBER

On 17th February 1923 the work in the first chamber of the tomb was finished. At last the excavators could open the sealed door between the antechamber and the burial chamber. The entrance was guarded by two large wooden statues. After the arrival of the invited guests, Carter managed to make a hole in the dividing wall with a hammer and chisel. Stone after stone was carefully removed. The guests watched nervously. They saw that Carter was faced with what seemed to be a solid wall of gold. The onlookers were amazed. But soon the riddle of the 'golden wall' was solved. Immediately behind the door of the burial chamber there were gigantic gilded shrines – immense wooden chests, covered in gold, to protect the king. The mummy of Tutankhamun had to be in there.

Carter and Carnarvon wriggled past the enormous wooden shrine and began to investigate the burial chamber. Had robbers disturbed the king in his eternal sleep? Impatiently Carter and Carnarvon pulled the bolts of the large shrine. The doors swung open. Inside the first shrine was a second one with an intact seal on the bolted door … The men sighed with relief. The mummy of the king must be untouched. Very carefully, they closed the door of the outer shrine for the time being.

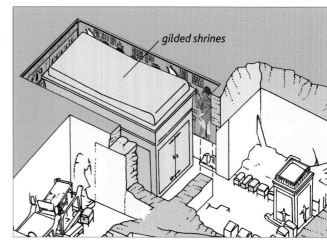

gilded shrines

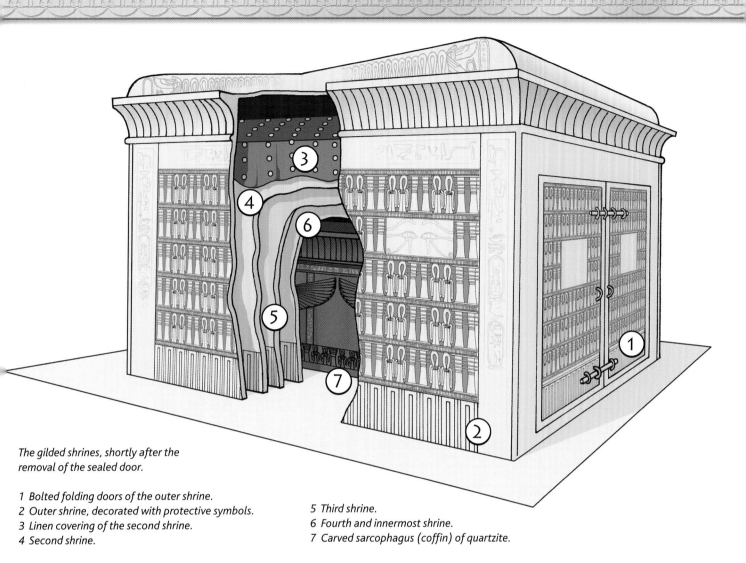

The gilded shrines, shortly after the removal of the sealed door.

1 Bolted folding doors of the outer shrine.
2 Outer shrine, decorated with protective symbols.
3 Linen covering of the second shrine.
4 Second shrine.

5 Third shrine.
6 Fourth and innermost shrine.
7 Carved sarcophagus (coffin) of quartzite.

THE TREASURY

At the end of the burial chamber, however, there was another surprise for Carter and Carnarvon. In the light of the lamp a small treasury became visible. A statue in the shape of a jackal, placed on top of a wooden chest, protected the entrance of a room beyond the burial chamber. A linen cloth was knotted around the neck of the animal. In the room were many boxes containing textiles, jewellery, ointments, cosmetics and other objects. A few bows and a number of model boats had also been given to the king. The most impressive object in the treasury, however, was the beautifully decorated gilded shrine that held the viscera (the intestines, stomach, lungs and liver) of the deceased king.

The jackal-god Anubis guarding the treasury.

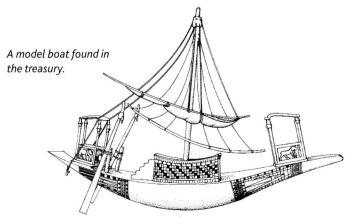

A model boat found in the treasury.

THE SIDE-CHAMBER

As well as the antechamber, the burial chamber and the treasury, the makers of Tutankhamun's tomb had also carved out an annexe or side-chamber to the antechamber. This small room was full of objects which were incredibly jumbled up. Wooden beds, chairs, three-legged stools, footrests, gaming boards, weapons … In the past robbers had also been here, searching for valuables. Chests and baskets had been opened and their contents thrown on the floor.

Also, provisions had been stocked in this room which the king could use in the afterlife. When clearing out the room, Carter found numerous baskets with roast fowl, nuts, fruit, seeds and various jars of wine.

The mummy of the king.

1 *Royal sceptres (flail and crook).*
2 *Golden dagger.*
3 *Protective bird, representing the king spirit.*
4 *Golden bands with hieroglyphic texts*

THE CURSE OF TUTANKHAMUN

'It is over, I have heard his call, I will follow him …' It is 5th April 1923. The Earl of Carnarvon lies delirious in a hotel bed in Cairo. The English nobleman has become very ill from an infected mosquito bite. He suffers attacks of high fever and cold sweats. Several times, Carnarvon utters the name of Tutankhamun. Tutankhamun … the young king from times long past. The pharaoh whose tomb he discovered together with Howard Carter. Tutankhamun … Carnarvon witnessed the opening of his burial chamber. With his own eyes he had seen the many treasures in the tomb … Tutankhamun …

Then suddenly Cairo is thrown into darkness. By the time the power failure is over, the Earl of Carnarvon is dead. The nobleman, who was so eager to open the shrines and coffins containing the mummy of Tutankhamun, never got the chance to come face to face with the king.

The news of Carnarvon's death travelled fast. His sudden death and the power failure fuelled the wildest rumours. People said that the earl had been struck by the curse of the pharaoh, and that Tutankhamun had taken his revenge on the man who violated his peace.

AN EXCITING JOB

Howard Carter was shocked by the death of the Earl of Carnarvon, but he was determined to finish the job. In October 1923, the archaeologist started to work on the shrines in the burial chamber. Carter needed to remove a total of four gilded casings without damaging them. This was not easy because the burial chamber was very small. Once the outer shrines were removed, Carter could see that the walls of the burial chamber were colourfully painted with scenes of Tutankhamun's funeral.

When the last shrine had been opened, the researchers discovered a large sarcophagus (a stone coffin) made of yellow quartzite. The granite lid of the sarcophagus was still in place. On 12th February 1924, the heavy lid was lifted from the sarcophagus with great care.

In the tomb, the guests waited nervously. While the lid of the sarcophagus hung above his head, Carter chanced a first look into the great stone sarcophagus. There was a coffin in the sarcophagus, a coffin of gilded wood, shaped like a mummy. Still the archaeologist had not reached the mummy of the king …

THE MUMMY OF THE KING

Carter studying the golden coffin of Tutankhamun.

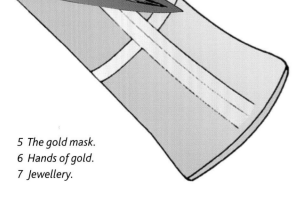

④ After a delay caused by a quarrel between Carter and the Egyptian government, the Englishman began the salvage operation again on 25th January 1925. The lid of the first coffin was lifted, revealing a second coffin of gilded wood. The second lid was also removed and slowly the third and last coffin became visible. This coffin surpassed all expectations. Finally, underneath cloths of fine linen and flower wreaths, Carter saw the gleam of solid gold. Dazzling! He had finally found the coffin that held the mummy. It was made of solid gold and weighed 110 kilograms. The lid was lifted by the handles and the mummy of the king was seen for the first time in over three thousand years. Carter had been looking forward to this moment for so long. The face of the king was covered with a golden mask.

5 The gold mask.
6 Hands of gold.
7 Jewellery.

THE END

On 10th November 1930 the last objects were removed from the tomb of Tutankhamun and brought to the laboratory. For ten years Howard Carter had worked on salvaging and recording the beautiful treasures. At last, in the spring of 1932, the last objects were transported by train and ship to Cairo. There, many objects from the tomb of Tutankhamun are still on display in the Egyptian Museum.

MAKE A MODEL OF TUTANKHAMUN'S TOMB

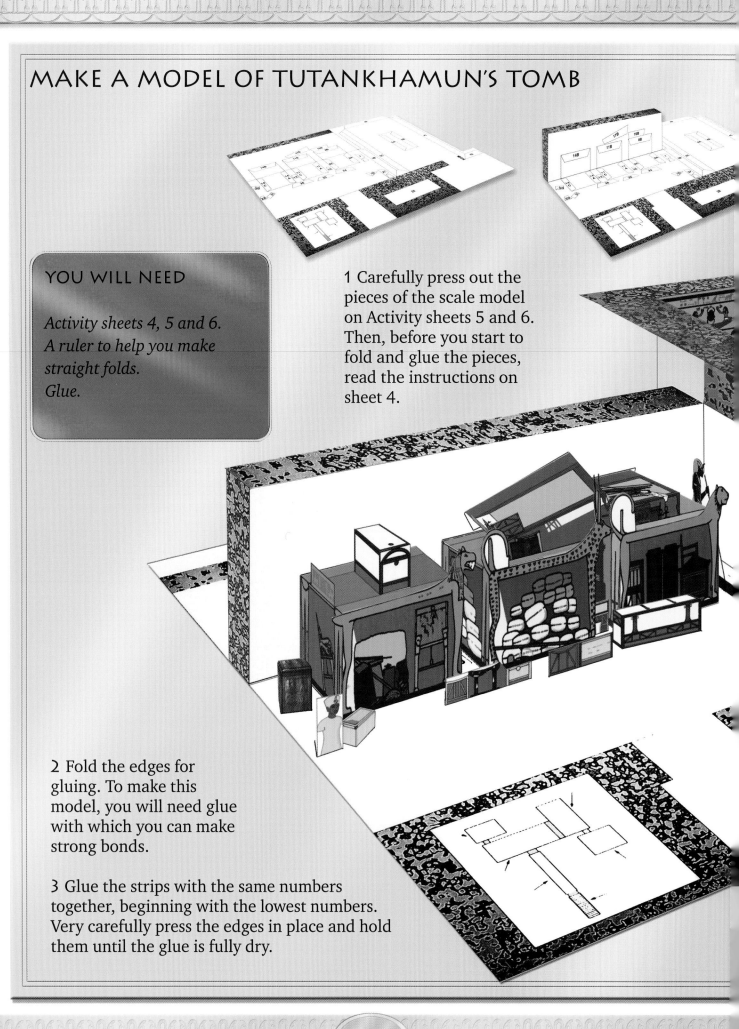

YOU WILL NEED

*Activity sheets 4, 5 and 6.
A ruler to help you make
straight folds.
Glue.*

1 Carefully press out the
pieces of the scale model
on Activity sheets 5 and 6.
Then, before you start to
fold and glue the pieces,
read the instructions on
sheet 4.

2 Fold the edges for
gluing. To make this
model, you will need glue
with which you can make
strong bonds.

3 Glue the strips with the same numbers
together, beginning with the lowest numbers.
Very carefully press the edges in place and hold
them until the glue is fully dry.

4 On Activity sheet 4 are a number of objects from Tutankhamun's tomb. Press them out carefully and fold the edges to be glued. The scale-models can then be glued together and put in the tomb. The numbers on the tomb floor show you where each object should go.

HINTS

• When folding the model pieces, use a ruler to help you make neat, straight folds.
• When gluing, take care to follow the instructions and drawings on Activity sheet 4.

TUTANKHAMUN'S WARDROBE

A tunic from Tutankhamun's tomb, decorated with red and blue rosettes and hieroglyphs. There are also falcon's wings around the neck.

HUNDREDS OF PIECES OF TEXTILES

In the tomb of Tutankhamun, Howard Carter discovered various treasures. As well as the gilded furniture, impressive wooden statues and golden objects, the young king had a large collection of textiles in his grave.

Carter and his fellow workers found hundreds of pieces of cloth, including rolls of linen and complete garments. The textiles were scattered over the entire tomb. Some pieces were lying on the floor, and others were knotted around statues. Yet other materials were stored in large wooden chests with neat labels. In fact, it was a real mess. Someone had disturbed the king's tomb …

A DANGEROUS JOB

Nervously the men look around them. They are on their guard. Are they being followed? Quietly they sneak in the direction of the rocks. Then they light their torches. The flames form small patches of light in the darkness. Concentrating hard, they get to work. Hammers and chisels appear from leather bags. With firm blows the men try to make a hole in the white plasterwork in front of them. The hieroglyphs of a king's name are dimly visible: Tut-ankh-Amun. They work briskly. Pieces of chalk are flying around. Suddenly one of the workers nudges the others. The hole is big enough to crawl through. One by one the men disappear. They need their tools. There is the sound of copper on stone again. Then muffled cries can be heard. They are inside the royal tomb. They have made it!

Hurriedly they search for valuables, grabbing precious golden objects. The men rummage through baskets and boxes, throwing the contents on the floor. Parts of a gilded throne are broken off and stashed in their bags. They also collect jewellery and pieces of valuable linen. Suddenly the sound of excited male voices penetrate through the tomb area … The tomb guards are coming! The robbers grab their loot and run for their lives.

Tomb robbers.

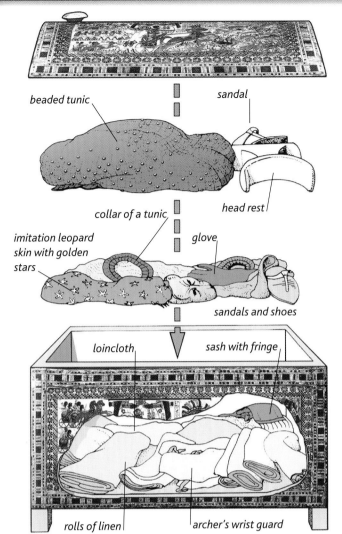

beaded tunic
sandal
collar of a tunic
head rest
imitation leopard skin with golden stars
glove
sandals and shoes
loincloth
sash with fringe
rolls of linen
archer's wrist guard

The contents of Tutankhamun's painted box.

A HURRIED TIDYING JOB

The managers of the royal cemetery must have been informed of the theft from Tutankhamun's tomb. They immediately started an investigation, but we do not know if the robbers were caught.

Next it was the task of a selected group of people to repair the damage to the tomb of the king. The 'cleaners' must have worked very hurriedly. They made no attempt to sort and replace the objects from the emptied chests and baskets. Instead they gathered up things by the armful and quickly put them away wherever they would fit. The textiles in particular were carelessly folded and put away in any convenient place. For example, walking sticks and linen underwear, and important garments and headrests, ended up muddled together in one box.

THE TEXTILE FINDS

When in 1922 the excavators started to remove the textiles from Tutankhamun's tomb, it soon became clear that some pieces of cloth had decayed so much that they could hardly be touched. Much damage had been caused by the 'cleaners' of the tomb. Also, water had seeped into the tomb in some places. As best they could, Carter and his fellow workers tried to treat, describe and photograph the pieces of textile. But it was not until 1992 that the clothes from the tomb of Tutankhamun were investigated scientifically.

REPLICAS

The examination of the clothing of Tutankhamun has supplied a lot of information. With the help of photos, notes and computer techniques the researchers have succeeded in tracing the original colours, woven decorations, and bead and embroidery patterns. It was even possible to reproduce a large part of Tutankhamun's wardrobe.

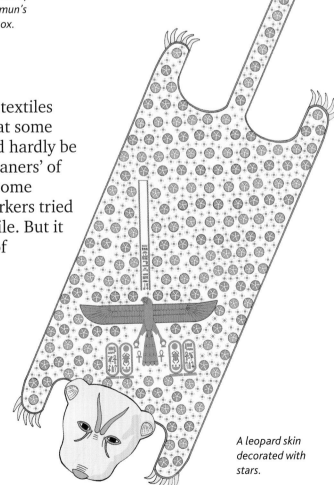

A leopard skin decorated with stars.

ANCIENT EGYPTIAN FASHION

Egypt is in northeastern Africa. It is very dry and hot. The ancient Egyptians mainly wore light linen clothing. Linen was made from the fibres of the flax plant grown on the banks of the Nile. The Egyptians wore simple garments, such as wraparound dresses, kilts, sashes, tunics and loin cloths, and they were usually white.

Women often wore dresses in ancient Egypt. The wraparound dress was easiest to make. This dress consisted of a long piece of material which was wrapped around the body one to three times. Sometimes women used two pieces of material which were tied together or were kept in place with a sash. Kilts were worn by men. A piece of cloth was wrapped around the lower body and held in place by a sash.

Tutankhamun wears a kilt and his queen Ankhesenamun a linen dress. They are shown dressed like this on the golden shrine in his tomb.

Sashes are long, narrow strips of material used to hold another garment in place, such as a loin cloth or a kilt. If the sash was very long, it was wound around the waist more than once. The sashes discovered in Tutankhamun's tomb sometimes ended in long red ribbons. They were often beautifully decorated. For instance, the king had sashes with flower motifs or with his own name embroidered.

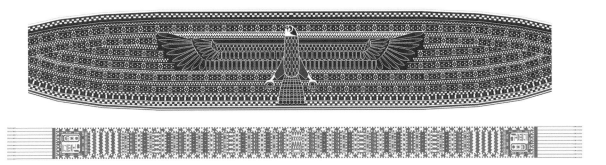

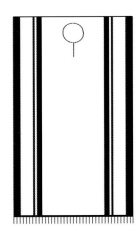

Egyptian tunics were bag-shaped. They were worn by both men and women. To make a tunic, the ancient Egyptians folded a rectangular piece of cloth in two. Then they sewed the sides together. In the centre of the upper fold, they cut a hole for the neck with a slit in front so that the tunic would go over the head ... and that was that!

A tunic from Tutankhamun's tomb.

Egyptian underwear was a simple loin cloth - a piece of linen wrapped around the waist, pulled between the legs and tied at the front with laces.

THE CLOTHING OF TUTANKHAMUN

Many garments were found in the tomb of Tutankhamun. Carter noted that Tutankhamun had 145 loin cloths. Perhaps the king thought that he would need all these items of underwear during his eternal life after death! Carter and his colleagues also found several tunics in the tomb. A number of them were once beautifully decorated with coloured beads, gold discs or woven or embroidered pictures. For example, the young king must have worn white tunics with blue and red stripes, rows of geese or hunting scenes. Also found in the tomb was a tunic with a woven pattern of falcon wings. These were meant to protect the king.

Carter also found several gloves and even various pairs of socks. It is possible that Tutankhamun used the undecorated gloves when riding in his chariot, and wore the fine, decorated gloves on ceremonial occasions.

Ay, Tutankhamun's vizier, wearing gloves.

MAKE YOUR OWN EGYPTIAN TUNIC AND SASH

Dress up in your own Egyptian tunic. You can make a tunic and sash from old sheets or bedclothes. But ask permission first!

Take a large piece of plain white sheet. Cut a neck opening in the centre, with a diameter of about 10 cm. Make a slit of about 10-15 cm at the front so it will go over your head easily.

Sew together the edges of the tunic, but don't forget to leave openings for the arm holes.

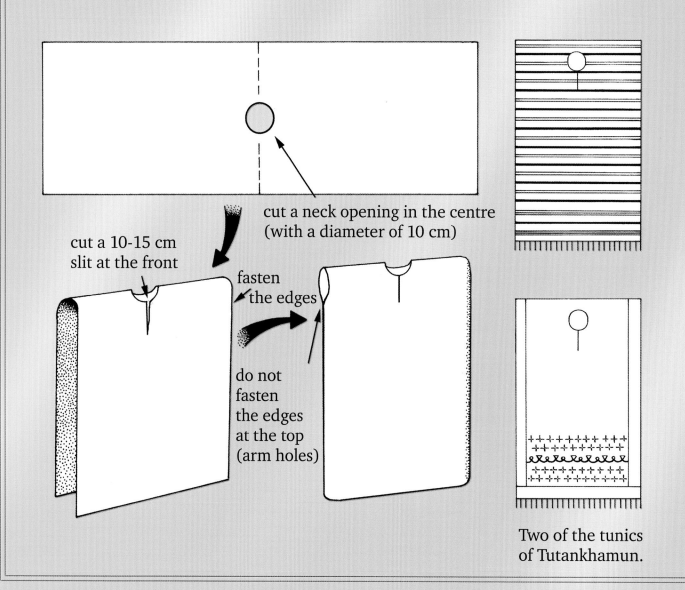

cut a neck opening in the centre
(with a diameter of 10 cm)

cut a 10-15 cm
slit at the front

fasten
the edges

do not
fasten
the edges
at the top
(arm holes)

Two of the tunics
of Tutankhamun.

For the sash, cut a long strip of white sheet. You could sew some fringes on to the short ends of the sash.

When your tunic and belt are ready, you can decorate them with coloured pictures and patterns. Use textile dye and a brush (take care!).

Activity sheet 7 shows different decorative patterns from Tutankhamun's own clothes, or you can copy other patterns and pictures from this book.

HINTS

• To decorate the clothes, use a brush and different colours of textile dye.

• You can copy the patterns of Activity sheet 7 or invent your own based on Egyptian pictures and colours.

• Wear slippers or sandals. Perhaps you can add a black wig, earrings or a bead necklace.

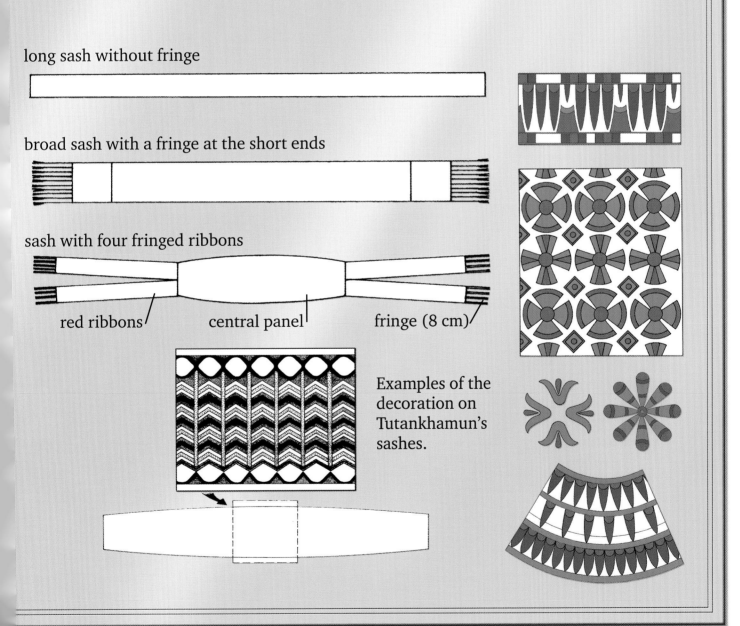

long sash without fringe

broad sash with a fringe at the short ends

sash with four fringed ribbons

red ribbons   central panel   fringe (8 cm)

Examples of the decoration on Tutankhamun's sashes.

SHOES, HAIR AND BEAUTY

THE SANDAL MAKERS

They are working hard in the tannery (a workshop where animal hides are made into leather). In a week's time a large quantity of sandals has to be delivered to the palace. The men know that the king checks everything and therefore they work very carefully. In a corner of the workshop one of the tanners is busy cleaning the hides and skins of cattle, goats and sheep. The remains of meat and hair tumble to the ground at great speed. In another part of the workshop, the hides are put in a pot with alum (a kind of salt mixture) for soaking. The sandal makers know from experience that this is a good way to make the hides water-repellent and to protect them against decay. After the men have taken the hides from the oil-like liquid, they lay the hides out to dry for a while. Then the hides are stretched on frames so that they can stretch out sufficiently and become supple. Other sandal makers are cutting soles out of the leather. They pierce holes in the soles to which the sandal straps are fastened. On long racks there are already dozens of pairs of sandals ready to be delivered.

Sandal makers in ancient Egypt.

FOOTWEAR FROM TUTANKHAMUN'S TOMB

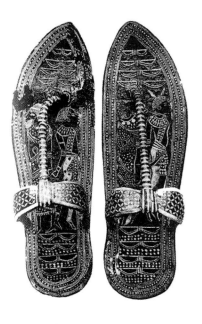

A pair of sandals of Tutankhamun with pictures of two tied-up enemies on the inside soles.

Footwear was an important part of the clothing of the Egyptian king. Ninety-three sandals were found in the tomb of Tutankhamun! Ancient Egyptian sandals were often cleverly decorated and they could be made of very different materials. In the royal tomb Howard Carter discovered sandals of leather, but also plaited ones. These plaited sandals were made of strips of palm leaf which had been wound around bunches of grass or papyrus. Some pairs even had a layer of gold leaf on the plaiting. A very special find was a pair of wooden sandals which were covered with green leather, tree bark and gilding. On the soles of these sandals you can see some bows and two tied-up enemies. So when the king wore his sandals, he was trampling on his opponents! After all, the king was powerful and vanquished all his enemies.

WIGS

Egyptians also gave much attention to their hair. Young children had the easiest 'hairdo': their heads were shaven apart from a long lock of hair over their right ear. Their parents often wore wigs, and certainly when they went to parties. Their own hair was usually shaven as short as possible. The wig protected the head against the strong sun.

Most wigs were made of wool or human hair. A skilled wigmaker knotted and plaited the hair and then secured it, according to the latest fashion, onto a base of fine netting or flax thread. The wigs were often decorated with jewellery, flowers, combs and pins. Sometimes a perfumed ointment cone was worn on the wig. The ointment slowly melted so that the wigs and the clothes of the ancient Egyptians were covered with a lovely-smelling grease.

The Egyptians used combs of wood, bone and ivory to disentangle the hair on the wig or to remove pests such as lice and ticks. When the wigs and hairpieces were not being worn, they were kept in special boxes or baskets. In this way the wigs kept their shape and they were protected against dust. Carter found such a wig box in Tutankhamun's tomb. The wooden box was magnificently decorated with blue and yellow inlay. In the centre of the chest, the woodworkers had made a mushroom-shaped support. This enabled the wig to hang freely in the box. Unfortunately the box in Tutankhamun's tomb was empty, but a few hairpieces were found in his tomb.

An Egyptian man's wig.

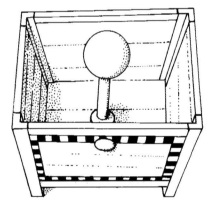

The wig box found in Tutankhamun's tomb.

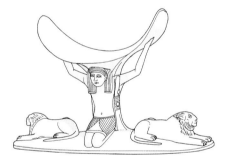

An ivory head-rest, used instead of a pillow.

Party guests wearing fine clothes, wigs and jewellery.

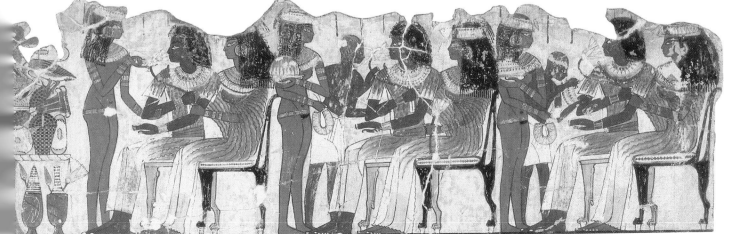

A ROYAL BATH

The young Tutankhamun is taking a bath. The bathing women have poured one jar of perfumed water after another over him. A lovely smell spreads through the room. The king is dried with fine linen towels. Then it is time to rub his body with oil. Servant girls are running to and fro. One of them has just opened a lovely decorated box. Carefully she displays a number of small alabaster vases and checks the labels: sesame, juniper, almond and olive oil. In order to make the oils smell good, extracts of all kinds of flowers, herbs and spices have been added. A massaging woman rubs it into the body of the king. The oils perfume his skin and make it soft and supple.

Next it is the turn of the servant girl to make up his eyes. With a small, thin gold stylus she applies the black eye-paint. Red blushes appear on the cheeks of the king. For this, the girl crushes some ochre (a red powder) and mixes it with a little fat. Then one of the girls hands the king a polished bronze mirror. Tutankhamun studies his face. His eyes look brighter because of the black eye-liner, and the red colour on his cheeks makes him look fit and healthy. The king is satisfied.

Necklace with a pectoral (a decorated piece that hangs over the chest).

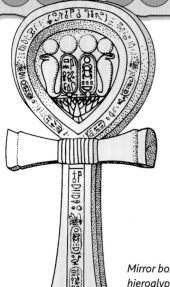

Mirror box shaped like the hieroglyph 'ankh' (meaning 'life', as well as 'mirror').

HYGIENE AND COSMETICS

Both Egyptian men and women used eye-paint. Black was the usual colour. The eye-paint was not only to make their eyes look brighter and bigger. By applying the paint, called kohl, around the eyes, they could reduce the glare of the sun. Sometimes they also coloured their eyelids with a green paint. Lips and cheeks were coloured red. Men and women used mirrors of polished copper, bronze or silver.

Toiletry articles, including a kohl stick and a cosmetic dish in the shape of a duck.

Many toiletries were found in Tutankhamun's tomb. Apparently the king also wanted to make himself look good in the life after death! The jars of kohl for black eye-paint, pots of ointments and perfume vases from the tomb are made of stone, metal, wood or ivory. In order to keep the toiletries safe and tidy, they were stored in decorated wooden chests with sliding lids or in wicker baskets.

Ointment jar with a lion on the lid.

A gold earring.

JEWELLERY

Without his or her jewellery, an Egyptian did not feel fully dressed. Rich men and women in ancient Egypt wore diadems, wig decorations, necklaces, pectorals, bracelets and anklets, earrings and rings. Wealthy people wore jewellery of valuable metal decorated with precious stones. Poorer Egyptians had to content themselves with beads of earthenware or faience. Because Tutankhamun was the king, the most precious materials were used for his jewellery. Goldsmiths worked many hours in their workshops to make the most splendid objects of gold, coloured glass and different kinds of semi-precious stones. Howard Carter must have been bowled over when he discovered the magnificent jewellery in Tutankhamun's tomb. Pectorals with pictures of different goddesses, necklaces with winged scarabs (a sacred beetle), earrings shaped like falcons with duck heads … no effort was spared to provide the young king with the most splendid adornments. Today we can still marvel at the wealth and splendour of the young king.

Falcon jewel found in the tomb of Tutankhamun.

Activity sheet 8, colouring pencils or felt-tip pens, glue, string and some sticky tape. You may also want paint or coloured paper and scissors. To finish your Egyptian look, you could use a black eye-pencil, green eye shadow, lipstick and blusher.

MAKE YOUR OWN EGYPTIAN JEWELLERY

Make an Egyptian pectoral to hang around your neck. Carefully press out the pectoral on Activity sheet 8. You can colour it in, paint it or glue pieces of coloured paper on to it. Ask an adult to make the holes for you, then hang the pectoral around your neck on some string.

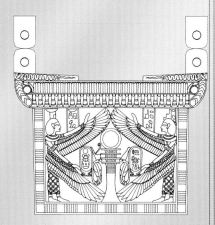

On Activity sheet 8 you will also find a bracelet. Press out the bracelet. Colour or paint it in Egyptian colours to create your own design. When you have decorated the bracelet, you can roll it around your wrist. Use sticky tape to join the ends.

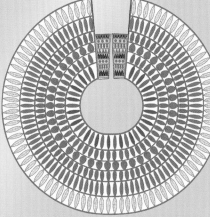

A broad collar of beads, from Tutankhamun's tomb.

These two party guests and the servant girl are wearing pectorals in the shape of broad collars.

HINT

You can give yourself an Egyptian make-up to go with your jewellery. With an eye-pencil or black make-up draw black lines around your eyes. Use green eye-shadow for your eyelids. Your lips can be reddened with lipstick.

(Remember, don't use anybody else's make-up without their permission!)